Ecosystems

Tundras

by Nadia Higgins

Bullfrog Books

Ideas for Parents and Teachers

Bullfrog Books let children practice reading informational text at the earliest reading levels. Repetition, familiar words, and photo labels support early readers.

Before Reading

- Discuss the cover photo. What does it tell them?

- Look at the picture glossary together. Read and discuss the words.

Read the Book

- "Walk" through the book and look at the photos. Let the child ask questions. Point out the photo labels.

- Read the book to the child, or have him or her read independently.

After Reading

- Prompt the child to think more. Ask: Have you ever visited the tundra? Have you seen videos or pictures? How would you describe it?

Bullfrog Books are published by Jump!
5357 Penn Avenue South
Minneapolis, MN 55419
www.jumplibrary.com

Library of Congress Cataloging-in-Publication Data

Names: Higgins, Nadia, author.
Title: Tundras / by Nadia Higgins.
Description: Minneapolis, MN: Jump!, Inc., [2017]
Series: Ecosystems
"Bullfrog Books are published by Jump!"
Audience: Ages 5–8. | Audience: K to grade 3.
Includes index.
Identifiers: LCCN 2017000802 (print)
LCCN 2017002383 (ebook)
ISBN 9781620316825 (hardcover: alk. paper)
ISBN 9781620317358 (pbk.)
ISBN 9781624965593 (ebook)
Subjects: LCSH: Tundra ecology—Juvenile literature. | Tundras—Juvenile literature.
Classification: LCC QH541.5.T8 H54 2017 (print)
LCC QH541.5.T8 (ebook) | DDC 577.5/86—dc23
LC record available at https://lccn.loc.gov/2017000802

Editor: Jenny Fretland VanVoorst
Book Designer: Molly Ballanger
Photo Researcher: Molly Ballanger

Photo Credits: Alamy: Scandphoto, cover; Radius Images, 4; Accent Alaska, 8–9. Biosphoto: Pierre Vernay/Polar Lys, 20–21. iStock: AlexeyKamenskiy, 11. Minden: Donald M. Jones, 12–13; Ingo Arndt, 18–19. Shutterstock: Maksimilian, 1; Dan Bach Kristensen, 3; JoannaPe, 6–7; Iakov Filimonov, 14; Alexander Erdbeer, 16; r.classen, 23tr; Nordroden, 23bl; Leonid Ikan, 23br; FotoRequest, 24. SuperStock: Wouter Pattyn/Buiten-beeld/Minden, 5; Matthias Breiter/Minden, 10; Eric Baccega/age fotostock, 16–17.

Printed in the United States of America at Corporate Graphics in North Mankato, Minnesota.

Table of Contents

Cold and Windy

A tundra is a cold place.

Winds whip.

No trees grow.

Most tundras are
in the Arctic.

They are flat.

Some are on
mountains.

Winter is long here.
Snow covers the land.

Summer is short.

The snow melts.

But not all of it.

Plants are low.

They grow in clumps.

They keep out
of the wind.

Animals need to stay warm. They have thick fur.

fur

Look! This bird has feathers under its feet.

They protect it from the cold ground.

feathers

Food is hard to find in winter.

Some animals go away.

They come back in summer.

Others rest.

They wake up in summer.

The tundra feels alive.
But the harsh cold
will soon return.

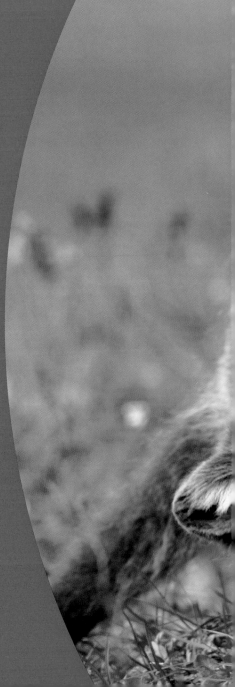

Where Are the Tundras?

Tundras are the world's coldest places. They cover about a fifth of Earth's land. Antarctica is cold, but it is not a tundra. It is a cold desert covered by a solid sheet of ice.

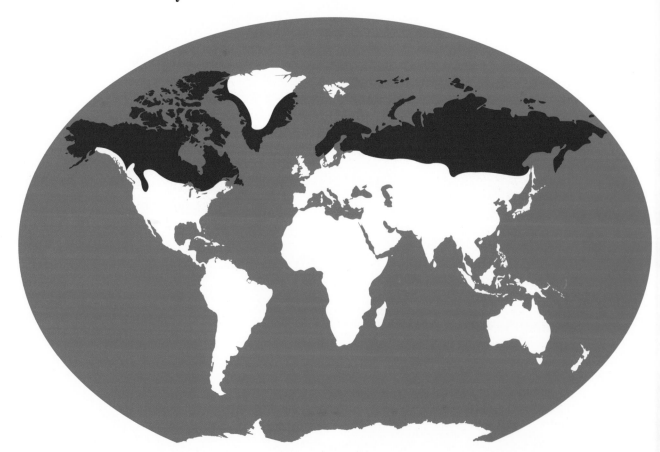

■ tundra

Picture Glossary

Arctic
The coldest part of the world that surrounds the North Pole.

melts
Changes from a solid to a liquid state due to increased temperature.

clumps
Thick groups.

protect
Cover or shield from something that would destroy or injure.

harsh
Making many or difficult demands.

whip
Move fast in one direction.

Index

To Learn More

Learning more is as easy as 1, 2, 3.

1) Go to www.factsurfer.com

2) Enter "tundras" into the search box.

3) Click the "Surf" button to see a list of websites.

With factsurfer.com, finding more information is just a click away.